Out of Darkness Into the Marvelous Light

Dr. Shell Moore PhD

Copyright © 2018; 2019 Dr. Shell Moore PhD

All rights reserved. No part of this publication may be reproduced, distributed, or transmitted in any form or by any means, including photocopying, recording, or other electronic or mechanical methods, without the prior written permission of the publisher, except in the case of brief quotations embodied in critical reviews and certain other noncommercial uses permitted by copyright law.

ISBN-13: 978-1-951300-98-2

Liberation's Publishing LLC
West Point, Mississippi
www.liberationspublishing.com

Out of Darkness Into the Marvelous Light

Dr. Shell Moore PhD

Out of Darkness

Introduction 7

Church Comes First 11

Not the perfect Family 17

Where Is The Ideal Family 21

God Will Not Forget 25

My Father The Model Pastor 27

I Couldn't Hide It 31

Experiencing the Supernatural 35

Searching The Scriptures 40

Financial Transition 45

A Time of Greater Testing 49

Bitter-Sweet Situation 57

He Will Guide Me 67

Conclusion 101

About the Author..................................... 103

Dr. Shell Moore PhD

Introduction

I was brought up in the very small town of Bruce, Mississippi. The largest town near it is Oxford, Mississippi, and it's known to most travelers. I am number thirteen out of fourteen siblings born to the late Ben and Ruby Williams.

We didn't have the best of housing however we were comfortable. I sometime think we lived that way, because we hadn't been introduced to a better lifestyle. I can remember having to put pots on the floor because of the leaks in the roof. I will never forget the outhouses (outdoor toilets). The hog killing days were epic; We cut up fat back and cooked crackling (skins). Let me not forget to mention the wrangler tangle washing machine. I've done my share of hand washing clothes.

I can remember those long garden rows that kept us fed. As for our personal needs, many neighbors would bring clothing to my parents. Our town officials would even give us the left over Christmas parade items.

My older sisters and brothers worked for an attorney. Each year when the attorney and his family did their spring cleaning they would send us their kids old toys. Many of the toys ran by batteries and were in good shape. One of my favorite toys was a go-car that he gave my brother.

Mind you We are a family of thirteen. I know now that the favor of God was and is still upon our lives. God is working all the time. Even when we don't understand, He is working. I do believe my father knew it was

Out of Darkness

God providing for us and showing us favor.

Dr. Shell Moore PhD

Church Comes First

During that time there were three black churches in the community that I knew of. There were the Methodist, Baptist, and Pentecostal. I belonged to a Pentecostal church also referred to "the Sanctified Church or the Holy Rollers".

The sanctified church was known for its shouting, dancing, and singing. Oh, yes and its testimony services. Those were the days when the anointing of God flowed and people were healed and lives were changed. The word of God was being preached according to Mark 16:20 where it says, "And they went forth and preached everywhere. The Lord was working with them and conforming the word with signs."

That kind of anointing is still available

today. If the signs are not following, it could be that the pure Gospel is not being preached; Mark 16:17-18 says, that these signs will follow those who believe. In Jesus name we shall cast out devils and speak with new tongues. We shall take up serpents; and if we drink any deadly thing it shall not hurt us. We shall lay hands on the sick, and they shall recover.

I know this to be true, as God stated in Jer.1:12 Then said the Lord unto me, Thou hast well seen: for I will hasten my word to perform it. When the unadulterated word is preached God is in the mist. People will be set-free and delivered.

Healing is very common. I had the opportunity to be trained by some of the greatest men and women of God. I long to be a part of that kind of atmosphere again. Being raised in the Pentecostal area was the greatest training of my life. I was blessed to watch my father and mother serve several pastors faithfully in the Church of God In Christ before they were appointed as pastors.

God's word says, Train a child the way it should go (Prov:22:6) The word of God is the solution for our young people today. Parents must model the word of God. "No ma'am, No Sir" is how we always responded to our elders. My parents did not send us to church without them, nor did they leave us at home. They carried us to church, and we were on time. They were the parents and they were in charge.

It is very important to train your children

in the nurture and admonition of the Lord. I was blessed to have saved parents, I KNOW. They reared us according to the best of their knowledge believing they were led by the Holy Ghost. We were trained to respect God's people, obey leadership, if someone had a title we addressed them accordingly. This is the first lines of training. Teach our children to submit to authority in our churches and schools. It begins in the homes.

My Mother taught us girls how to carry ourselves. We were taught how to cook, clean house, can food, wash, iron, dress, and set the table. We were taught how to carry ourselves around young men. Mom taught us how to dress, about personal hygiene, and how to do our hair. My Father took care of our brothers. I remember him saying to them that a man is responsible for his family. He must provide food, shelter, clothing, insurance, transportation, and always pay their bills.

Our family had orders and boundaries. The wife should only work if she wants to. Yes, my mom was a beautician. I just want to make it plain He wasn't saying anything against the wife choosing to have a job or career. My father solely believed that the family is mainly the man's responsibility.

My father strictly believed what the word said that the husband is the head of the wife, even as Christ is the Head of the Church; and he is the savior of the body (Eph:5:23). He modeled what he taught. Oh yea, you would rather for him to whip you because mom never got tired and dad whipped fast.

Not the perfect Family

However, as any family we fussed, fought, lied, and stole from each other just as any ordinary family would. We played games such as hopscotch, London bridges, hide and go seek, Simon says. Yes, you know we played Church and I was the pastor.

The name of My Church was "This is the Church of what happens now." This too became a training for us both naturally and spiritually. However as children we didn't know it at the time. We sang, shouted, and mocked the saints dances. If we got in trouble we would be discipline as in most black families the discipline was way more severe than the situation. I know in this 20th century those whippings would be labeled as abuse. Maybe my parents based their discipline literally on (Prov:23:13) "Withhold not correction from the child: for if thou beatest him with the rod, he shall not die." Well we didn't die, we survived.

I think a lot of my mother's frustrations steamed was because of her life not being fulfilled. I was told by my mom that I reminded her of her mother's side of the family. There was a line of women pastors, preachers, and bishops that she was originally part of. The organization originally honored women in these positions but not anymore.

I often wondered if she harbored resentment in her because she knew that she had a greater calling on her life; but She was not allowed to carry it out due to the new denominational doctrine that she had become a part of. They did not honor women in these positions.

I have heard her say she could see her passion for ministry life fulfilled through me, as well as other women that were in ministry. I often think back on some of the whippings, bruises, and negative remarks that we as sibling endure. The whippings were for little things, underserving of beatings. Sometimes we might have needed a whipping, but it is a difference between abuse and whipping.

I still thank God for my parents being Godly parents as much as they understood. When I was a child , I spake as a child, I though as a child: but when I became a man (woman) I put away childish things. (1

Corinthians 13:11)

I know now we was just a real family that had wrinkles, spots, disappointments. We had goals that seemed unattainable. We had expectations for ourselves as well as others that might have been unrealistic. Looking at things from a child's eyes. Thank God we know now that we are more than a conqueror Romans 8:37.

Where Is The Ideal Family

The scriptures will help us understand that the Bible does not present ideal families. Take a moment to read Colossians3:18-21:

8 Wives, submit yourselves unto your own husbands, as it is fit in the Lord.

19 Husbands, love your wives, and be not bitter against them.

20 Children, obey your parents in all things: for this is well pleasing unto the Lord.

21 Fathers, provoke not your children to anger, lest they be discouraged.

There is also a passages in Ephesians 5:21 through Chapter 6:4; and the book of Proverbs that has been written aforetime for our learning for instruction as well as wisdom. There have always been difficulties in families from the Old Testament thru the New Testament. These words were written for our encouragement, edification, and instruction. The Apostle Paul writes to correct and prevent problems in Christian families. I am positive the writer of Proverbs has prevention of trouble in mind becoming known as the book of wisdom.

We can also receive encouragement that God had trouble with his family. The following names serves to remind us of God's conflict with his children: Adam and Eve, who had trouble obeying God and falling into temptation. This fall began a downward spiral for the family such as blaming others for our decisions. Adam blames Eve, Eve blames the serpent. There is the sibling rivalry of Cain And Abel. There is the father and son conflict of David and Absalom and so many more. The fact that God had trouble with his family teaches us that God knows what it feels like to have family difficulties. I thank God for being a God that knows how to deal with the family .

Dr. Shell Moore PhD

God Will Not Forget

I observed my father serving several pastors along with mom doing whatever she could to assist him. Mom and the other women would often work together to sell dinners to help meet the vows they had made. Faithful even before he became the senior pastor. Although, he was one of the original founders of this said church in Bruce, MS. He still made sure the church had what it needed.

We would have the pastors and their families over for dinner and have more than enough. I watched this man and woman of God with thirteen children put God first and God favor was upon their lives. We eventually got a brand new home no more (out house) and we were blessed with nice cars. I watched God bring us from a mighty long way. Observing my parents and being faithful to God's word has also instilled a greater level of faith in me. I knows the word works.

My father served God and the church leaders faithfully. I believed my father served under four pastors at least before God touched a pastor from Batesville, MS who was serving at this time and told him it was time for him to turn the church over to Elder Williams. The Superintendent agreed. The proper channel was followed and my father was ordained the Pastor.

My Father The Model Pastor

My father, the pastor, believed in and modeled Timothy 4-5. One who rules well his own house, having his children in subjection, with all gravity for if a man know not how to rule his own house, how shall he take care of the church of God?

We had to go to all of the services and do whatever it took to make things come together. I thank God for that now. We were trained how to conduct all facets of the services according to the doctrine. We were also known as pastor kids as well (hint hint). Although, we were reared in the same setting each of us formed our own personality.

I was drawn to the word. I would have dreams of someone teaching me as she writes on the board. I remember in one dream she drew a human body and began to label it as she pointed to parts of the body. She said as to the body of Christ there are many members but one body as she referred to 1 Cor. 14-27. I came to realize that it was the will of God for me to know that he was bigger than denominations.

However, this denomination laid the foundation that I still stand on. Holiness is right and I find no fault in it. When the Word sounded sometime incomplete, I would pick up my Bible and highlight what I did not understand. I would find myself praying and asking God, "Why do I have this great desire to know more about this topic?" I did not realize at the time that the gift of teaching was within me.

Out of Darkness

Later on in life, as I continue to establish my relationship with Christ. The lady in the vision was actually me in the spiritual realm. I later on became a seminary professor, and I do draw on the board and teach as the woman in the dream did in many setting.

Dr. Shell Moore PhD

I Couldn't Hide It

When I entering high school, my senior year I fell in love with a young man (David). I got pregnant. We got married, and I move to Houlka, MS. I told myself no more church. I did continue to come back to Bruce through the week to finish my senior year out and I graduated Shell Denece Williams Moore class of 1978.

Nevertheless, not knowing the calling of the Lord was upon my life was on the inside. I told myself being raised in the church, I am going to make my own decision now I am not going to church. I begin to dream about church. I was in church services. My husband would shake me and ask me what are you doing? You are preaching in your sleep. I can remember on one occasion we had a waterbed. I had stood up in my sleep and began to walk in the bed preaching and teaching. However; my husband to amazing awakening woke me up again pulling me down to the bed. I know at this time my husband did not know what to think about the situation. I thank God for his patience and kindness towards me.

Well, the longing to be in the presence of God started again. I started going to revival at a Pentacostal church in Houlka, Mississippi where I received the Holy Ghost. I then went back home to my home church in Bruce, MS and began to diligently work in the church there. God also began to manifest other gifts that he was imparting in my life such as laying on hands and praying for people. I also began to flow in the prophetic. It wasn't long before God began to elevate me to be teachers and president over different auxiliaries .

Dr. Shell Moore PhD

Experiencing the Supernatural

Come let me share some personal experiences hoping that you all might explore this supernatural journey with me with a spiritual insight allowing the holy spirit to guide you (1 Cor. 2:14). But the natural man received not the things of the spirit of God: for the are foolishness unto him.

From a child supernatural events happened in my life. I would have visions, that I first thought were dreams. I saw people and described them to my mom, and she would tell me who they were. I could see into the future. I would describe events or places as a child of six or seven. Many times I would lay in bed seeing spirits, and I often saw angels.

I recall a telephone conversation I had on a landline phone. After we hung up she said some very negative things about me to whoever was there with her. I waited for them to finish talking. After they had finished I called her back. I let her know I heard them talking about me, and asked her why she said what she said.

Her first reaction was to hang up, but in a few minutes, she called back. She said she never would have believed it if she hadn't experienced it herself. They both got on the phone and asked forgiveness. God in his awesomeness had already conditioned my hearts to forgive them as well as search my own heart. This was the beginning of getting acquainted with one of God wonderful gifts.

The supernatural power of God never

ceases to amaze me. Yes, I know many of God's people do not believe in the power of God to this extreme. Having a form of Godliness but denying the power thereof (2 Tim. 3:5 I know his power beyond speculation. Having these experiences with God has given me a clearer revelation of the written word of God and how his powers operates. As it was then and still is now in most congregations. We are in the need of God-fearing mentors.

God began to use me in the ministry in the gifts of prophecy. When I asked for guidance I was just told I was strange and many times made a mockery of. It did not matter that the things I prophesied by the Holy Ghost came to pass. They could receive these prophecies or words of knowledge/wisdom but it is common to be rejected by your own.

I learned quickly what Mark 6:4-5 meant, Jesus said, "A prophet is not without honour but in his own country and among his own kin and in his own house. And he could there do no mighty work save that he laid his hands upon a few sick folk and healed them."

I noticed in these verses that Jesus works were limited because of the unbelief of the people. I was encouraged to find out the problem was not that he could not do mighty works but their attitudes toward his works limit them from being blessed.

As God began to visit me in visions, I began to search the scriptures to discover who I was in the Lord and to know my purpose. I found out God knew me even before I was born (Jeremiah 1:5). Before, I formed you in the belly I knew thee; and before thou camest forth out of the womb I sanctified thee and I ordained thee a prophet unto the nations." Wow, I now began to understand the foreknowledge of God. He knows who we are.

Searching The Scriptures

The Lord launched a thirst in me to search the scriptures. Just like any other process, studying and submitting myself to the word of God prepared me for a greater purpose. It was the studying and commitment to the will of God and not my will.

God continued to allow me to minister where I was often misunderstood facing the pain of rejection many times. However Teaching was and is my passion. Although, I was often hurt and misunderstood in my home church, God had graced me with an unstoppable anointing. I held several positions such as secretary, teacher, and was president of several auxiliaries. Many times, I would be viewing a situation one way, but it was being received completely opposite. Yet, I still had to stay focused and put my trust in God .

God graced me with the passion to study the word of God with a deep desire to know him "not by might, nor by power, but by my spirit said the Lord (Zech.4:6). I have seen leaders walk in power, but the power was many times questionable. Many of the situations I was being challenged with took much prayer and trying by the word of God (I John 4:1). You see I knew some of the things I was experiencing wasn't right. I needed to know how to differentiate the spirit or spirits that were in operation (I John 1b) but try the spirits whether they are of God.

I was appointed the Elect Lady of a district and I will be forever grateful to that District

Missionary. This was a great experience However it wasn't long after the pastor began to take sick and things began to change. I know things are subject to change when different leaders are in charge that is to be expected. However, that is not what I am talking about.

My dad took sick and another great man of God stepped up. My baby brother stepped up and did the best he could. I didn't understand many of the changes or mixed signals being sent such as being accused of things. To this day I knew it was not true. This is when I came to realize that whatever a person believe is their truth. I would be told to do certain things and when I would get to church somebody else would be doing it. It wouldn't be mentioned.

Out of Darkness

There was a time when I went to my office and another person came in to inform me that she had been appointed part of my job. I remember saying, I am sorry, and I was not told. When I inquired about it I was simply told well you know now. I want you to understand it wasn't the changes that were so out of order it was the way things were being handled. The bible says let all things be done decently and in order (1Cor.14:40).

This is where I now believe God began to prepare me for the transition. Just as an Mother Eagle prepares her eaglets to leave the nest she began to make things uncomfortable for them by moving the sticks out of the middle of the nest. Then she takes her strong beak and feet and breaks the sticks and stand them straight up in the middle of the nest. She is determined to get them to their full potential. Because after all the eaglets has a great Eagle that is developing to soar to greater heights and deeper depths.

Financial Transition

Mom and Dad didn't understand business when the church account was set up by them. At that time the membership was very small. They put their finances that were raised on special anniversaries into the church account to help sustain the church. However, when dad got sick the younger generation did not understand that and things did get uncomfortable.

My mother was asked to sign the account over to the church and they agreed to give her a small percentage. This was somewhat painful for mom as well as myself having to write up the papers for this transition. Dad had not passed at this time he was still in the hospital in Oxford, MS. Let me say, I do believe with good intentions and everybody meant well (Proverbs 21:2). Every way of a man is right in his own eyes: but the Lord pondereth the hearts."

I tried to stay faithful seeing the hurt in Mom's eyes and not understanding what was going on at this point myself. I tried to talk to the pastor asking what is going on? The answer would be "you know." I tried to talk to the leaders and the answers would be "submit to authority."

Let me pause and thank God right here for the power of the Holy Ghost (comforter, helper, advocate, Counselor, strengthener, Guide, standby). I notice that what I was saying was not being heard as a cry for help. I wasn't looking for anyone to take sides. I needed a spiritual counselor, someone that wasn't so caught up in positions that they couldn't see the conditions. I was looking for someone to sit down and talk to me and give me some Godly instructions.

I could not find the Spirit of Counseling in the house. However, I did come to this conclusion as in (Psalm 16:7) I will bless the Lord, who has given me counsel: my reins also instruct me in the night season. This transition helped me to learn obedience and trust (Rom. 8:28). And we know that all things work together for good to them who love God, to them who are called according to his purpose. This statement means exactly what it says according to God's purpose not ours.

This situation began to make me very uncomfortable not being able to find a counselor in this situation. I have always had a special love for this great man of God and for Satan to be allowed to come between us, I just couldn't believe it. Let me warn somebody right here the power of influence is powerful, rather it is money, fame, jealousy and etc. and can blind people mind to true situations and realities.

A Time of Greater Testing

My father, the pastor, passed away. My brother was then appointed the senior pastor wonderful right. I watched my mom being dishonored. I watched her heart being shattered. I watched my mom being stripped of all her pride. Someone even said directly to me that my mom was hurting because she was losing her power as the first lady. This could have been a beautiful transition if it would have been handle correctly. However, I have came to know many times people are doing the best of their understanding.

What do you do when what you love is making you feel bitter? I wanted to stay because this is where I grew up. These people seemed like family. Many of us grew up together and were saved under the same leadership. We had worked together for many years. In so many ways dealing with what it seemed to be a tug-of-war in the spiritual realm also felt like I was experiencing a type of death. Many time I would get to church and be addressed with situations that really shocked me. I wondered what caused the body of Christ to set out to want to believe the worst about their sister and brothers (Revelations 12:10b).

I believe it showed a great need for maturity and the love for God (Matthew 18:15-17). If your brother shall trespass against thee, go and tell him his fault between thee and him alone: if he shall hear thee, thy hast gained thy brother. Many time statements were made that seemed to have been directed toward myself or mom. Yes, again in the best way that I knew how I tried to make sense out of the situation. I even told myself you could be hearing things wrong because you are already experiencing a great transition with your dad being sick and the other things that are going on.

My husband often advised me not to go back. However; something down on the inside would say not yet (1John 4:b) because greater is he who is in you, than he who is in the world). God does things decently and in order. By the time the next service would come my husband would say we can go back if you want to. Since, I knew that God had not released me we continued to go to the services.

Many times I attempted to bail out to

avoid rumors that seemed to out weight the truth. I thank God for saved parents. My mom would often say "Shell you just do what is right and God will do his part." The problem here it seemed to me that it would have been easier to walk away than to suffer through it. However, I quickly found out life wasn't fair. II Timothy 2:12-13) if we suffer we shall also reign with him. If we deny him he also will deny us. If ye believe not yet He abides faithful. He cannot deny Himself."

I had to encourage myself in the Lord. I began to find scripture that I felt in my heart was the counsel of God. I came to know the most critical test that one will ever face is the test of suffering when in your heart when you are trying to do what is right. Blessed are they who are persecuted for righteousness. But if ye suffer for righteousness sake happy are ye : and be not afraid of their terror, neither be troubled.

Through this ordeal I learned a life time lesson, people have a tendency of following their geographical order of understanding. He that answered a matter before he heareth it, it is folly and shame unto him (Prov:18:13) I am not talking about praying people. I am talking those that are swift to pass judgement on others. I know this statement sounds bitter mainly because it is from a bitter seed which is called pains of disappointment.

Mom was still living at this point. I wanted to leave and I wanted to stay knowing she was still dealing with Dad's death and the changes. I was also being stripped of my positions as well, and with no explanation. Many times we say we don't care and deeply on the inside we are spiritually broken when there is no explanation to changes.

One might ask me what does this have to do with preparing to unmask. You see so many of God people are denominationally save. They refuse to adhere to God's saying anything any different than what they expect. We often hide behind masks and try to blame everybody else for our preparation. I know now this is where I was at that time. I didn't understand God was preparing me for my transition. We often blame the devil or somebody when we do not understand how God is working. So, let's just unmask and say I have been hurt by the situation and God help me to be real with myself so I can be healed.

Dr. Shell Moore PhD

Bitter-Sweet Situation

You see it was a bitter-sweet situation. Mom was still hanging in there hurt and it seem as though her hurt was taken for bitterness not understanding her fight within. My roots was there and God hadn't released me yet. Mom and I were getting ready to go to a Valentine's Day Banquet in Shannon, MS. I was the keynote speaker. I was talking to mom on the phone while I was getting ready.

I had shared with Sister Stovall earlier that morning the Lord had spoken to me and said your mother do not have long. I shared with my mother during our conversation that the Lord loved her much. I do remember her having short breaths while we were talking not realizing this would be our last conversation.

Right after we hung up my husband (David) went to pick her up. He wasn't gone five minutes before the phone rang Mom had fell dead. She was fully dressed for the banquet in her beautiful red outfit. It was on February fourteenth Valentine's Day.

I told myself I am leaving as soon as the funeral is over. I am so glad God knows us he again gave me a desire to be still a little while longer. I was told by some that I should start my own church. I do believe people see gifts in people and do mean to be an encouragement many times. There is that pressing need to wait on God's timing. I had the gifts, but God needed to heal the hurt and show me the bitterness in me toward the situation. That bitterness had to be resolved before I could be used by him.

I came to understand that the importance of our spiritual wellbeing mentally and spiritually in many cases tends and does play a great role in our psychological mentality. We must stay focused on the kingdom in order to stay balanced and remember to stay whole. We are not designed to stay operating only on the soulish level. I got a new car and on my dashboard, it keeps track on my wheels pressure. Anytime the wheels loses pressure my dashboard notifies me. When I'm traveling and the atmosphere changes my wheel pressure changes. I have to put air in my tires. Just like my wheels, our life is that way.

Sometimes, in our lives we ignore the signs of things becoming imbalance. We must watch the signs of and immediately put them in check. Many times, there are changes in our life, but we don't pay attention to the atmosphere. We can tell the ride has become bumpy, but we ignore it. Not understanding that other things are being destroyed because we didn't stop and regain balance.

Repent and Forgive to Begin the Healing Process

I needed to repent and forgive. While I was in the house I could not change the atmosphere but I could change my perception. I cried out for God to help me and to will my mind to repent and to forgive, and to help me let go of the pass. By me calling out to God, he refilled me allowing me to regain balance. I asked God to do it just for me once again.

However, after realizing in my hurt and painful situation, I came to realize my soul was in trouble. This is where the self-consciousness resides. This is the area known as self. Where our will and affection lie in which are influenced by the understanding of our hurt and pain that we are in in that time. However, in my hurt and pain I was pushed to a place of studying where the word of God allowed the spirit of god to overrule my soulish realm. The spirit is a realm where the God consciousness resides, which causes the soul to transform.

The spirit of man is the candle of the Lord searching all the inward parts of the belly. (Out of your belly shall flow rivers of living water). It took God in me and spending time with him allowing my soul to revolve around God's word. As his word began to reign in my spirit the transformation began. This caused my heart to link up with my spirit and soul. My mind always wanted to be there, but my heart was broken and shattered. This caused my heart to link up with my spirit. I had the knowledge, but I did not have the will. (the spirit is willing, but the flesh is weak) Only then can we become the fruitful Christians that we are called to be. Although we may still make mistakes, let us say they are the price for a fruitful life. If we learn from them. I noticed in 1 Cor 12:28-30 there are two occurrences of the phrase gifts of healing. I also noticed that the word gifts and healings were plural, so I came to realize that God wants to heal his people soul, body and spirit. We do know that we as humans are made in the image of God, but because of the fall, our minds were the most damaged. Before the fall our minds was perfect. We had one Lord until Satan presented himself as such, and we chose to listen to another God. We were manipulated and Satan is using the same method today. The body of Christ must realize that the battle began in the Garden of Eden. It was to control our mind. The body must realize that spiritual formation is the process whereby we become equipped with the necessary tools to fully develop our soul spirit and body to become unified towards glorifying God honestly.

Your mind, heart, and spirit has to come into agreement, until then we see forgiving as the beginning of the healing process. Forgiving also frees a person to receive from God. Forgiving is letting go of the resentment and bitterness toward the situations or individuals. It is a joint effort with the holy spirit. I also learned through this process that God was also preparing me for transition as well. God healed me in this situation I began to look at things from a different perspective. My heart open up an my soul was renewed and now the right spirit is allowed to work within me. The love for my church family and forgiveness toward my Pastor was renewed and things began to work out fine. God's Word is a lamp and Light (Ps:119:105)

Out of Darkness

God's word began to reveal to me the main mask that I was wearing was a mask of tradition. I assumed because I was reared up in this denomination I would surely be there until I die. I would quickly quote (Romans 8:28) And we know everything work together for the good to them who love God (the first condition), to them who are called according to His purpose.

I had to come in agreement with God's purpose and not mine. (Which is the second condition). Let this mind be in you which was also in Christ Jesus. God had already given me a mind to search the scriptures. I hadn't even realized he was preparing me for the shift .

Dr. Shell Moore PhD

He Will Guide Me

I was lead to enroll in a school of Christian Counselor. In these classes the word of God was and the only tools used. The scriptures spoken in faith in the name of Jesus, has awesome power to overcome all obstacles. Psalm 107:20, "God sent his word, and healed them, and delivered them from their destruction."

I learned from this experience the damage that can be done to a person if he/she miss diagnosed in one of our services. We are quick to label people as acting strange, can't we talk? Do you really know what's going on with your sister/brother? Ever problem is not demonic. Everybody is not just being ugly? So many of us have master alternative personalities because we are afraid of the bullying in the church arena. Example of bullying *trying to explain to someone what you are going through. Many times we get very negative responses I already knew it such as God has already showed me. Sometimes, every answer seem to be negative rather than encouragement. Constructive criticism may be needed sometimes but let's be careful to not become a critics (Proverbs 12:25).

During my healing process God taught me how to differentiate between many issues. Enrolling into Christian counseling courses was to my advantage. The issues that I didn't know how to explain finally came to light in one of the courses that I studied. I believe many members of the body of Christ could be diagnose with this if they would be true to themselves (Psychosomatic illness). This is a combination of two Greek words psyche (or, soul) and soma (or, body). This illness is real and painful it is describe as bodily ailment that is caused by a maladjustment in the individual's' soul life [or originating from a mental, or emotional problem] rather than from the body itself. Christian counselors also use another term pneumosomatic disease-from pneuma (spirit), and soma (body). What I am describing is a lack of proper adjustment within the individual's spiritual life whose manifestation affects the whole persons in their soul and their body, although the real source of the problem is often deeply spiritual.

When I was going through this transition I also became somewhat ill. I visit the doctor he could not find anything physical wrong with me according to the X-ray machine. After taking courses in Christian Psychology, I became familiar with the terms psychosomatic and pneumosomatic. Some of the symptoms are lack of sleep, chest pain, headaches, and anxiety. These are some of the experiences that I was having. Now I know my problems was deeply spiritual.

The studies in schools began to help me understand the pain as well refocused my mind. The bitterness is now gone. I now understand that I must allow the word of God to bring me out of this dark spot and balance my life. I could feel the holy ghost restoring my mind "And being renewed in the spirit of my mind "(Eph 4:23).

I may not be able to give you all the formulas for success, but I can give you the correct formula for failure and that is trying to please everybody and that do includes yourself. Through fasting and praying the God of wisdom is now in charge. I am now more focus on his will and not mine. I did continue to go to bible college, and worked in the district and fell back in love with my church family.

This became a very productive time of growth mentally, physically, spiritually. God kept me still until it became about his purpose and not mine. He helped me develop a nevertheless mind toward many situations. God taught me how to truly forgive in spite, of and to love in the name of Jesus. There are many members in the body of Christ that hide behind masks as well as many have alternate personalities and will never be who they could be in Christ unless they confront the real person. Know this you are unique and God loves you. You are so important he created you in his image take of the mask.

Many times in life we will have to suffer for righteousness sake. I am not saying I made all the right choices, but thank God he knew my heart and my intentions were not malicious. Man judges the outer appearance or outer actions but God judges the heart (Isaiah 6:7). For man looketh on the outer appearance but the God looks on the heart. So many times we misses our blessings by looking for certain types of people and making our choices and labeling it or assigning God's name to that choice.

Let me encourage those who feel or know for a fact that you are looked over, remember that man can appoint people but only God can anoint them. The church is crying out for the anointing of God in this season.

If you are feeling discourages remember this, God did not make a mistake when he chose you. Although, the enemy through rejection, disrespect, etc. oftentimes, make us believe we have missed God in many situations. Remember this God words said "For I know the thoughts that I think toward you, said the LORD, thoughts of peace, and not evil, to give you and expected end

(Jer.29:11)." I hope I have established that God have a plan for your life and he had not change his mind.

I realize pain/fear oftentimes, manipulates our choice, we must admit no one choses pain and likes it. As we continue to explore this book some keys will be given. Let me share with you pain, rejection, shame, and many other factor causes people to layer themselves with false and mixed emotion. However, let me tell you it is okay to be real. Jesus have paid the price for everything we have and will go through. The finished work of the Christ is our victory over anything that comes against the word of God. Jesus was forsaken so you and I will not be forsaken (Matthew 27:46).

Eloi, Eloi, lama- sa-bach thani? That is

to say, My God, why have you forsaken me? He was made shame so you and I do not have to live in shame. Who his own self bear our sins in His own body on the tree, that we being dead to sins, should live unto righteousness: by whose stripes you were healed (I Peter 2:24b).

However, if we stay focus and realized that we are the righteousness of God because Christ has once suffered for sins, the just for the unjust. So we might suffer but its ok along as we suffer for righteousness sake.

I Peter 4:19 "Wherefore let them who suffer according to the will of God commit the keeping of their souls, as unto a faithful Creator. This is the guaranteed victory.

Dr. Shell Moore PhD

Strength to Unmask

When God set my mindset in order I had the strength to begin to unmask myself layer by layer. Know this some layers was harder, than other to pull off during my painful moments. I put on characters and attitudes that was assigned to me by my surroundings and circumstances. Each layer of pain disappointment etc. of life tends to form a personality as a type of protection mechanism which in reality can easily become a masked lifestyle, or alternate personalities.

I finally realized I can trust God with all of Me .It was me who needed to let myself out of those dark rooms in my soul and realize It was ok to know I am out of Darkness he has done for me WOW!!!

- He was punished that we might be forgiven.

- He was wounded that we might be healed.

- He was made a curse that we might receive the blessings.

- He was made sin with our sinfulness that we might be made righteousness with his righteousness.

- He died our death that we might share his life.

- And he endure our poverty that we might have life more abundantly.

Now learning these things let us continue to remove the masks that we are making payment on and wearing so uncomfortable.

Not realizing that they are already paid for and defeated in him. We can't buy what's not for sale. It is a done deal.

For in him we move and have our being (Acts 17:28). I now realize there is safety in the ark of covenant. I no longer have to wear a mask. Coming out with my focus on him. Rather, you are in a masked marriage or a locked heart or broken promises. God knows who you are where you are in Jesus is your answer.

Keys

• Christ is smart enough, wise enough, and very much qualify to separate who we are from what we have done or doing. We actually use more energy on self-hate than it take to turn from our sins. Remember God loves you unconditionally.

- Keys for a blessed marriage. Remember you must be aware that a normal marriage encounters three rings engagement ring, wedding ring, and the suffering.

- Understanding the strength of pain. Fearing the pain involved almost all of us to a greater or lesser degree often time we attempt to avoid problems. Sometimes, we procrastinate hoping that they will go away. We ignore them, forget them, or pretend they do not exist. We attempt to get out of them rather than suffer through them.

- Those who avoid their problems usually end up with more problems in the future. People who faces their problems usually save themselves a great deal of unnecessary suffering later on in life. Pray and be led by the Holy Ghost. Some situation you might needs to seek Wise Counsel.

- Self-deception is a slower killer of one's true identity and is a very compromising place to be in life. Remember this that lies produce death, truth produces life. There is a truth we learn from everyday life experience, there is just environmental truth, cultural truth, but to know the real truth that will be and is the most powerful and sustaining truth of all, We have to look beyond ourselves, our intellect, and skills of observation, and depend on God to reveal them to us. Because he knows us better than we know ourselves.

I would like to remind you that most of our emotional struggles, relationship difficulties, and spiritual setbacks are cause by the lies we tell ourselves and accepts from others.

As a Christian counselor, and as a Pastor, I believe the lie that I should be available for the people all time, any time. Now, I still believe availability is just as important as ability but with an understanding. In other words, I had to learn to take the mask off and learn when and how to say No when no is needed. "God called us to labor on His behalf to bear one another's burdens but we are told that each person is supposed to carry his own share of the load. I had to remind myself not to become so busy serving Christ people that I had not spend the time I needed to sit at the feet of Christ to be replenished or get help for myself. Acknowledge God in all your ways and he shall direct your paths

(Proverbs 3:6).

Strategy to Overcome Life Disappointments

- Its not just a get over it situation many times.

- You must start taking steps away from your pain by facing it and controlling it. Example: a baby learning to walk might fall, might stagger, might even cry, and be bruised but he is resilient which the ability to go through and knowing what you are trying to accomplish could and more likely bring more pain.

- Remember you can make it everything you needs to is in you (Romans 12:3). God hath dealt to every man the measure of Faith. You see faith is our key to accessing the full power of God. Faith provokes the heart of God and releases His wisdom, power and understanding, into any situation or circumstances.

- We must accept where we are and quit denying that we need help and stop developing a masks or behavioral to cover our true feeling or pains, concerning what really is in our hearts. Remember your body, your attitude, your friends that you are making, and other are paying the cost of the mask. You will now step out and trust God's word its ok he got you. Remember you must no longer rely on your understanding you must have faith in God and petition the throne of grace as to your next move.

- In all thy way acknowledge him and he shall direct your path Proverbs 3:6. Some of us engaged in all kinds of activities from prostitution, child molestation, murder, homosexual, lesbians, liars, whatever it is it seem that we substitute to assist our pain or for temporary acceptance. However, in the end there is NO peace.

However, we know these are temporary masks. Although, they may seem to be self-fulfilling but anything that exalt itself against the word of God will be casted down (II Corinthians 10:5a) and I can promise the secret ingredient is death. I know it feels good and sounds good to think we are really in control. But God who is rich in mercy for his great love where with he love us even when we were dead in sins hath quicken us together with Christ by grace ye are saved. And hath raised us up together in heavenly places in Christ Jesus. That in the time ages to come.

Once we accept or acknowledge the pain and trauma of life you just cannot stop your emotions or repress your feeling without your body counting the cost. Your body do not have any organs in it that is design or have the ability to carry stressed or emotions that is overbearing. Remember the word says to us come unto him all that are heavy laden and I will give you rest somebody says by the grace of the Lord I have come a long way.

All the sinful things we may have done or encounter Satan does not want us to know or really believe. Romans 5:20b But where sin abounded Grace did much more abound. You see unmerited favor is given to us by

God. Romans 3 what shall we say than shall we continue in sin that grace may abound God forbid. However, Grace is the power that enables us to endure and progress through many challenges. Paul reminded us that some things might I add even when removing the mask as in II Corinthians that some thorns in life will have to live with but God grace is sufficient. God's grace will undergird what we have to deal with. Some of the scare that some masks will leave imprinted in our lives. Somethings are left in our lives to keep up humble and remind us God is more than able to carry us through. Weakness causes me to be strong depending on God. I can do all things through Christ who strengthen me Philippians 4:13. II Corinthians my strength is made perfect in weaknesses. I learned through by the grace of God my strength was also developed. His strength allows us to stand in time of difficulty, heartache, resist temptation, and remain steadfast in him.

We must be reminded what God has called us to do is beyond our strength we must rely on his strength. The thing I have observed in the body of Christ is that we will not admit we need help to overcome. We have the tendency to create a behavior that cover the real pain. We hide behind anger, lies to others, and ourselves.

Let's began to remove the masks. First, let us confess where we are I John 1:9, "If we confess our sins, he is faithful and just and will forgive us our sins and purify us from all unrighteousness. I know many of our pains are inflicted by others and we sometimes allows pains to rule our minds as well as our life decisions. What do you hear me saying from this passage Psalms 66:18 If I have cherished sin in my heart the Lord would not have listened. I heard many say that they are praying but have not forgiven themselves or others. Unforgiving is a major sin that blocks many from getting their prayer request listened to by God as stated in Psalms 16:18.

Until we take the masks off and face ourselves we will continue to walk in darkness. Let me remind you that we cannot allow pass fear to control present our life when there is nothing we can do to correct the past. We must trust it to God's future care Isaiah 43:18. Remember ye not the former things neither consider the things of old. In others word you must cast our eyes forwards not backwards.

The enemy do not want us to focus on the deliverance plan that God have for us. He do not want us to know that we are forgiven just by repenting and allowing the love of God to be shed abroad in our heart. It is very simple Romans 10:9 says that if you confess with your mouth. Jesus is Lord, and believe in your heart that God raised him from the dead you shall be saved.

One might asked what happen once I have been saved. Salvation mean to be set free. This freedom free us from the bondage of the enemies of this world. You see Satan have loss his power over your mind.

Let us now draw near to God with a

sincere heart in full assurance of faith, having our hearts sprinkled to clean us from a guilty conscience and having our bodies cleansed by the word of God. For we are fearfully and wonderfully made Psalms 139:14B.

Let me help you through this transition for whatever mask you wore or is still wearing be aware that Christ came because of sin. Sin equal most pains and masks (or covering) not just that little sin that we often think nobody knows about even those open sin (transgression) and those filled with inward sin (iniquity).

Because of him (Christ) we now have a covering which is the blood of Christ which has the ability to make us white as snow. When we truly believe in the finished work of the cross and allow the word of God to transform our minds. I know many of us say if we cannot hide from God no need of trying to hide from nobody else. Let me put you on notice open sin is the same as open rebellion which lead to another level of disrespect. For example, some of us do not believe that it is a sin to smoke but we have enough respect for the house of God not to set in the pews and light up a cigarette and began to smoke. The word of God declares that rebellion is as the sin of witchcraft and stubbornness is as iniquity and idolatry. Because you have rejected the word of God (1 Samuel 15:23.); (respects goes a long ways).

One might ask why did I use such a powerful comparison because rebellion is another key factor that allows familiar spirits to control the mind that help many to create the masks of life and make decision. A person cannot and will not be genuine as long as he or she walk in rebellion and stubbornness.

I know some of us has been lead to believe its too hard to face reality and you are not strong enough to allow the real you out. I cannot control the real me and I am afraid to allow anything or anybody else deal with the masked me. The enemy do not want you to find out if you come out and allow God to fight for you his strength will be a very present help. The Bible say that Christ's strength is made perfect in weakness (II Corinthians 12:9b) and that he is the strength (Philippians 4:13).

Out of Darkness

I know the most of us attends church regularly. However, I wonder how many people have we caused to stumble or hinder from coming to Christ, because of the masks that we used in different situations. You do not have to be a drug addict, prostitute, gay lesbian, curser, or just have a plain bad attitude to wear masks. Some of us are known for just being a person of a comedian spirit trying to please everybody. We change with each crowd we have become affiliated with. We confused people when they hear us saying one thing but they see us living contrary to our profession. Some come even into those same setting where you have testified how God is and how you know him. But we come to service like we are on swing shift. Service starts at 10:00 A.M. am some of us shows up during different times or just before the messages.

We must admit we are not committed to God like we should be. We also must know the people you are witnessing to see your talk and your walk does not match. So guess what they know you wearing a mask. One way we know who or what you are committed to, is what your decide to do right towards. I am not talking occasionally. Doing what is right is the become lifestyle of a servant of God. It is no way we can love God and do not have respect for his house or for fellow Christians. Come on let's take off the masks so we can be free. Let face reality II Corinthians 4:3 says, "But if our Gospel be hid it is hid to them that are lost….When we do not take off our masks we cover the light and allow Satan to hinder your influence to those that need it most.

Remember only the pure in heart can be true to themselves and other (Proverbs 20:9). "Who can say I have made my heart clean, I am pure from my sin?" The answer is no one. It is a work that only accomplished by God. However, apart from God's word no Christian can live in purity. God's word is spiritual food. It nourishes, strengthens, and replenishes the soul. This is a daily need just as we nourished our natural body so is the same spiritual. Now, taking off the masks do not only allows what really in your heart to be dealt with. But it also allows God to remove the darkness. The light of God will unmask the indwelling will of God in your heart.

Dr. Shell Moore PhD

Unmask to be Armed to Win the War Within

When we pull off the masks of this world we can put on the armor of God Ephesians 6:11.

Wearing the mask will cause you to forsake the shield of faith which will leave you real vulnerable to the manipulations of this world. When we believers in the world system, over the word of God, we become a vessel of mixed revelation that leads to confusions and the devil invade our minds with his fiery darts, which is spiritual, physical, and emotional. It will not allow you to depend on God's word which transforms the mind over the matter that produce healing of the past that allow our minds hope to move into the future.

When we allow the devil to manipulate

our minds we cannot guard our mind with truth. We allow Satan to talk to us many time even through the word of God not knowing he can twist it to the way you want to understand it. He know where the mask is we cannot put on the breastplate of righteousness because many of the body of Christ have harden their heart as a form of protection from life issues. They often use this scripture as a mask (Prov. 4:23). Keep (guard) keep your heart with all diligence; make sure you are keeping it and you have not harden it. What in a man's heart guides him.

When a person's heart is not pure it cannot be guide with the preparation of the Gospel of peace in which our feet must be shod. Faith come by hearing and hearing come by the word of God without the proper Gospel your faith could be tainted. We as Christians can only have Faith in the finish work of the cross (Galatians 1:8)

The Gospel - if your faith level is handicapped by a tainted gospel than you cannot take on the shield of faith. The gospel of the cross is the only faith that God will recognize, and it is the only faith that have the power to quench all the fiery darts of wicked.

You see the devil realize if we don't take off the masks we cannot take on the helmet of salvation. This is where the mind is and it must be renewed Ephesians 4:22-23. That you put off concerning the former conversation the old man which is corrupted according to the deceitful lusts and be renewed in the spirit of your mind. Remember the old man wears masks but we have put him off. Now let take the sword of the spirit which is the word of God. This new man has the authority the unmasked man the one that no longer lives in darkness and prays with all prayer and supplication in the spirit.

We will pray until the prayer Is answered (Luke 18:1-8): Watching thereunto with all perseverance and supplication for all saints.

Dr. Shell Moore PhD

Conclusion

Let us pray for one another. We no longer wear masks we no longer lives in darkness. We now walks in the marvelous light.(Jeremiah 29:11). For I know the thoughts I think toward you, saith the LORD, thoughts of peace, and not of evil, to give an expected end. Just as I was trained in a certain denomination and honestly believed that my ministry was there for life. God had other plans. The (Holy Ghost) who searches the hearts knows what is in the mind of the spirit, because he makes intercession for the saints according to the will of God (Rom. 8:27). Remember we might miss God will but if we allow the holy Ghost to strengthen us the word of God will help us to be truthful to ourselves so we can unmask to withstand the warfare of the kingdom.

UMNMASKED BY THE WORD OF GOD

1Peter 2:9b…….out of darkness into His marvelous light.

About the Author

Dr. Moore is the co-founder of Jacksonville Theological Seminary Houston, MS branch. She was also an instructor as well as the Dean of Christian Counseling.

Dr. Moore played a major role in establishing Life Christian University-Institute, Tupelo, MS where she also became an Instructor.

Dr. Moore is the founder and director of Zoe Transformational Counseling Center located in Houston, MS.

Dr. Moore along with Elder David Moore is also the Overseer and Founder of Alpha and Omega Transformational Ministries, Houston, MS.

Dr. Moore is also the founder and director of

Dr. Shell Moore PhD

The Eagle of the Rose Scholarship Fund in honor of her parents the Late Elder Benjamin Williams and Mother Ruby Williams.

Dr. Moore also have an on-line curriculum where you can receive your Life Coaching degree from Sarasota Academy of Christian Counseling with direct contact with her and Dr. Duncan.

Dr. Moore states her most important accomplishment is she was born again and received the Holy Ghost in 1979. She has continued to travel the journey since then led by the power of the HG where she perceives to be the wisdom and director of all her studies.

Out of Darkness

Tribute

Tribute to the late Elder Sinatra Williams, my brother. He was a man of God after God's own heart, and left behind a legacy. He did an excellent work in the Kingdom with his wisdom, passion, and love he had for God's people. Rest in Peace. Well done,

Love always your sister

Dr. Shell Williams Moore, PH.D.

Dr. Shell Moore PhD

www.ingramcontent.com/pod-product-compliance
Lightning Source LLC
Chambersburg PA
CBHW060102230426
43661CB00033B/1400/J